This book belongs to

....

Dolphin Rescue and Other Stories

How this collection works

This *Biff, Chip and Kipper* collection is one of a series of four books at **Read with Oxford Stage 3**. It is divided into two distinct halves.

The first half focuses on phonics, with two stories written in line with the phonics your child will have learned at school: *Dolphin Rescue* and *Gran's New Blue Shoes*. The second half contains two stories that use everyday language: *Husky Adventure* and *Hairy-Scary Monster*. These stories help to broaden your child's wider reading experience. There are also fun activities to enjoy throughout the book.

How to use this book

Find a time to read with your child when they are not too tired and are happy to concentrate for about fifteen minutes. Reading at this stage should be a shared and enjoyable experience. It is best to choose just one story for each session.

There are tips for each part of the book to help you make the most of the stories and activities. The tips for reading on pages 4 and 28 show you how to introduce your child to the phonics stories.

The tips for reading on pages 58 and 88 explain how you can best approach reading the stories that use a wider vocabulary. At the end of each of the four stories you will find four 'Talk about the story' questions. These will help your child to think about what they have read, and to relate the story to their own experiences. The questions are followed by a fun activity.

Enjoy sharing the stories!

Contents

OXFORD
UNIVERSITY PRESS

Phonics

Tips for reading *Dolphin Rescue*

Children learn best when reading is relaxed and enjoyable.

- Talk about the title and the picture on page 5, and read the speech bubble.

- Identify the letter pattern *ph* in the title and talk about the sound it makes when you read it ('f').

- Look at the *ph, f, ee* and *ea* words on page 6.
  Say the sound then read the words (e.g. *ph – phone, ee – deep*).

- Read the story and find the words with the letter patterns *ph, f, ee* and *ea* in them.

- Talk about the story and do the fun activities at the end of the story.

Children enjoy re-reading stories and this helps to build their confidence.

Have fun!

After you have read the story, find eight starfish hidden in the pictures.

The main sounds practised in this story are 'f' as in *dolphin* and 'ee' as in *sea*.

 For more activities, free eBooks and practical advice to help your child progress with reading visit **oxfordowl.co.uk**

Dolphin Rescue

Can Gran save the dolphin?

Say the sounds and read the words

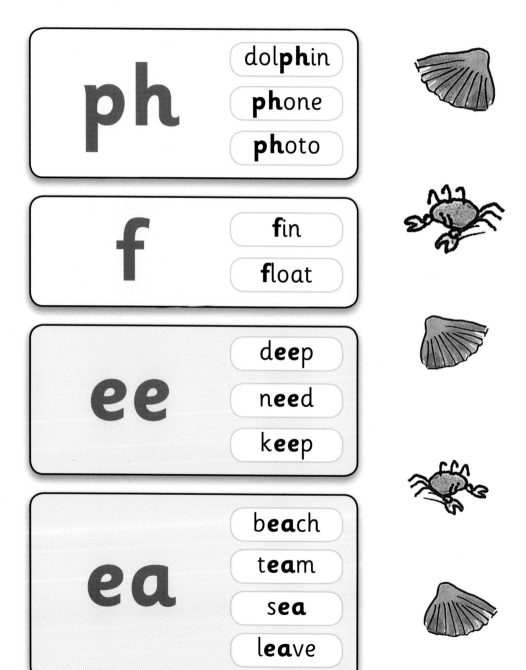

ph
- dol**ph**in
- **ph**one
- **ph**oto

f
- **f**in
- **f**loat

ee
- d**ee**p
- n**ee**d
- k**ee**p

ea
- b**ea**ch
- t**ea**m
- s**ea**
- l**ea**ve

A grey shape lay on the beach.

"Oh no!" said Gran. "It's a dolphin."
"Why is it lying there?" said Wilf.

"It has lost its way," said Gran.

"It needs to go back into deep water."

Some men got to the dolphin.

"Let's pull it back in the sea," said
a man.

Gran ran up to the men.

"No!" she cried. "Leave it alone."

"I will phone the dolphin rescue team," she said. "They will get it back into deep water."

Gran told Wilma to keep all the
children away.

"It is lying on its side," said Gran.
"Get it upright."

"Keep it cool," said Gran.

"It needs shade."

"Don't get water in the
blow-hole," said a man.

A man tried to take a photo of
the dolphin.

Soon the dolphin rescue team came.

The rescue team put the dolphin on a float.

The rescue team took the dolphin
back into the sea.

"I hope the dolphin will be all right," said Biff.

Talk about the story

Why did Gran phone the dolphin rescue team?

What did Gran and the men do for the dolphin?

What did the dolphin rescue team do?

Have you helped a creature in distress? How?

f or ph?

The sound 'f' can be spelled *f* and *ph*. Match the right 'f' spelling to the pictures and complete the word.

dol__in

_ish

__one

_loppy

ele__ant

Word jumble

Make the *f* and *ph* words and the *ee* and *ea* words from the story.

ee   s

i   f   n

p   k   ee

m   ea   t

n   d   ee   s

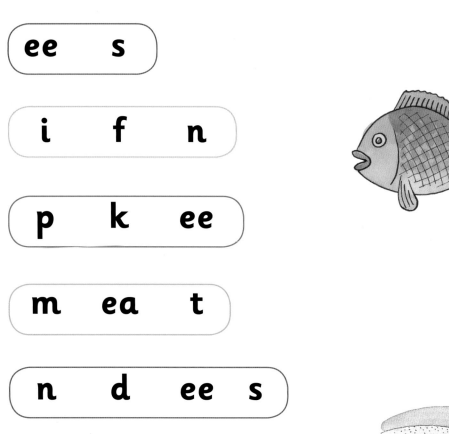

A maze

Help the dolphin find its way out to the open sea.

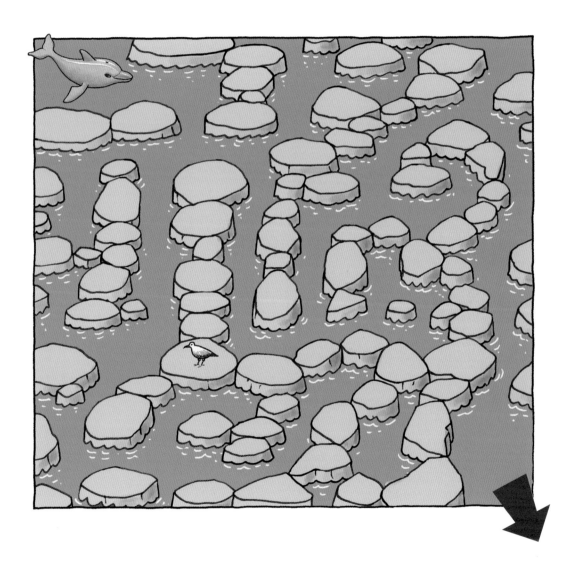

Tips for reading *Gran's New Blue Shoes*

Children learn best when reading is relaxed and enjoyable.

- Talk about the title and the picture on page 29, and read the speech bubble.

- Identify the letter patterns *ew* and *ue* in the title and talk about the sound they make when you read them ('oo').

- Look at the *ew* and *ue* words on page 30. Say each word and then say the sounds in each word (e.g. *drew, d-r-ew; true, t-r-ue*).

- Read the story together, then find the words with the letter patterns *ew* and *ue* in them.

- Talk about the story and do the fun activity at the end of the story.

Children enjoy re-reading stories and this helps to build their confidence.

Have fun!

After you have read the story, find the nine pigeons in the pictures.

The main sound practised in this story is 'oo' as in *flew* and *glue*.

For more activities, free eBooks and practical advice to help your child progress with reading visit **oxfordowl.co.uk**

Gran's New Blue Shoes

What will Gran do when the heel of her shoe breaks?

Read these words

n**ew**	dr**ew**
ph**ew**	tr**ue**
kn**ew**	gl**ue**
fl**ew**	bl**ue**

Mum had some good news.
"Gran is going to meet the Queen,"
she said.

A car drew up. It was Gran.

"I am going to meet the Queen,"
she said.

"Good for you," said Mum.

"What great news."

"I will need to choose a new dress ...
and a hat ... and new shoes," said Gran.

Gran got a new dress. She had a
new hat and new blue shoes.

The time flew by. At last, Mum
took Gran to London. Biff, Chip and
Kipper went too.

"The Queen lives here," said Gran.

Oh no! The heel on Gran's new, blue
shoe came off.

Gran was upset.

"I can't meet the Queen with no heel on my shoe," she said.

"I can lend you some blue boots,"
said a lady.

"I can glue the heel on," said a man.

"I have a tube of glue in my van."

A big car drew up. A flag flew on
the roof.

43

Chip ran up to the car.

"Stop that boy," called a man.

"Excuse me. Will you help us?"
called Chip.

The car stopped and a man got out.

It was the Duke.

"The heel has come off Gran's new blue shoe," said Chip.

"I'll see what I can do," said the Duke.
"Wait by this gate."

Later, a man came to the gate. He had a box. It was full of blue shoes.

"You can choose from these shoes,"
he said.

Gran went to meet the Queen.

"I do like your shoes," said the Queen.

"Gran's blue shoes will be big news," said Biff.

Talk about the story

What happened to Gran's new pair of blue shoes?

What was wrong with the blue boots?

How did the Duke help Gran?

What would you wear if you went to meet the Queen?

Rhyming words

Read each word on the blue shoe box.
Find a rhyming word on the red shoe box.

shoes   boot
blue   moon

flute   blew
prune   clues

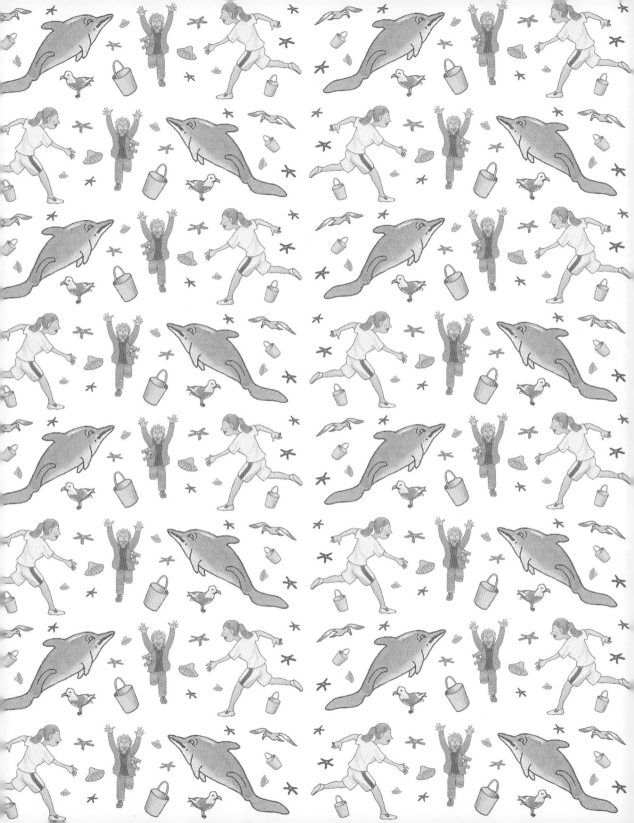

Stories for Wider Reading

Children learn best when reading is relaxed and enjoyable. These two stories use simple everyday language. You can help your child to read any more challenging words in the context of the story. Children enjoy re-reading stories and this helps to build their confidence and their vocabulary.

Tips for reading *Husky Adventure*

- Talk about the title and the picture on page 59, and read the speech bubble.
- Share the story, encouraging your child to read as much of it as they can.
- Give lots of praise as your child reads, and help them when necessary.
- If your child gets stuck on a word that is easily decodable, encourage them to say the sounds and then blend them together to read the word. Read the whole sentence again. Focus on the meaning. If the word is not decodable, or is still too tricky, just read the word for them and move on.
- When you've finished reading the story, talk about it with your child, using the 'Talk about the story' questions at the end.
- Do the activity on page 86.
- Re-read the story later, again encouraging your child to read as much of it as they can.

Have fun!

This story includes these useful common words:

thought   pull(ed)   fast(er)

must   suddenly

For more activities, free eBooks and practical advice to help your child progress with reading visit **oxfordowl.co.uk**

Husky Adventure

Can Floppy run as fast as the husky dogs?

It had been snowing. Kipper wanted
Floppy to pull his sled.

"Go on, Floppy! Pull!" he called.

Floppy didn't want to pull the sled.
He ran and hid in Biff's bedroom.

Suddenly, the magic key began to glow. It took Floppy into an adventure.

The magic took Floppy to a dark, cold
forest. There was snow everywhere.

The snow felt cold on Floppy's paws
and a cold wind was blowing.
"Brrrr!" thought Floppy.

Floppy began to walk, but his paws
sank in the deep snow.

He heard a howling sound.

AOOOOOW!

"What is that?" thought Floppy.

Oh no! It was a pack of wolves. They
had red eyes and long white teeth.
They growled at Floppy.

Floppy was scared of the wolves. He ran through the trees.

Suddenly, Floppy fell down. He rolled over and over. He went faster and faster.

Then he hit a tree.
BUMP!

Floppy lay in the snow with his eyes shut. A man ran up.

"Quick!" he said. "My boy is sick.
I must get him to hospital. I need
another dog to pull the sled."

The man took Floppy to the sled.
"Oh no!" thought Floppy. "Another
pack of wolves!"

But they were not wolves, they were husky dogs. The dogs growled.

"Are you the new dog? You look too floppy to pull a sled," they said.

The man put straps on Floppy.
"You've got to run fast," he said. "We
must get to the hospital."

The biggest dog barked at Floppy. "Just keep up, you floppy dog," he said. "We've got to run fast."

Floppy was cross. "Don't call *me* a
floppy dog," he said. "I'll show you!"

The sled went faster and faster.
"Slow down!" panted the husky
dogs. "We can't keep up with you."

At last, they got to the hospital.

"Thank you!" shouted the man.

"You've saved my son."

The husky dogs looked at Floppy.

"Wow! You can run fast!" they said.

"You're not a floppy dog."

"You can stay with us," said the
husky dogs. "We need a dog like you."

The magic key began to glow.
"Good!" thought Floppy. "I need
a rest."

"Come and pull my sled, Floppy,"
said Kipper.

"Oh no!" thought Floppy.

Talk about the story

Why did Floppy go and hide?

Did the husky dogs think Floppy would be good at pulling the sled? Why not?

Why couldn't the man take his son to hospital in a car?

Where would you like to go on a magic key adventure?

A maze

Help the dog team to find their way to the hospital.

Tips for reading *Hairy-Scary Monster*

Children learn best when reading is relaxed and enjoyable.

- Talk about the title and the picture on page 89, and read the speech bubble.
- Share the story, encouraging your child to read as much of it as they can with you.
- Give lots of praise as your child reads, and help them when necessary.
- If your child gets stuck on a word that is easily decodable, encourage them to say the sounds and then blend them together to read the word. Read the whole sentence again. Focus on the meaning. If the word is not decodable, or is still too tricky, just read the word for them and move on.
- When you've finished reading the story, talk about it with your child, using the 'Talk about the story' questions at the end.
- Do the activity on page 116.
- Re-read the story later, again encouraging your child to read as much of it as they can.

After you have read the story, find 21 mini monsters in the pictures.

This story includes these useful common words:
laughed   something   under   behind

Have fun!

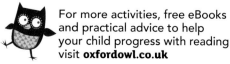

For more activities, free eBooks and practical advice to help your child progress with reading visit **oxfordowl.co.uk**

Hairy-Scary Monster

Who is the hairy-scary monster?

Kipper didn't want to go to sleep.
"Biff and Chip are at Gran's," he said.
"I don't like being on my own."

"Poor Kipper," thought Floppy. "I'll stay with him."

"Oh no, Floppy," said Mum. "Kipper is going to sleep."

But Kipper wasn't going to sleep. He was wide awake.

"I can't go to sleep," he grumbled. "I just can't!"

Kipper laughed. "I know! I'll play a trick," he said. "I'll trick Dad and get him to come upstairs."

He jumped up and down on his bed.
"Dad!" he yelled. "There's a hairy-
scary monster! It's coming to get me,
Dad. Help!"

Dad ran up to Kipper's bedroom.
Floppy barked and ran after him.

"What monster?" said Dad. "Where
is it?"

Kipper pointed to the curtains. "It's behind the curtains," he said. "It's got sharp yellow teeth and glowing red eyes."

Dad looked behind the curtains, but
he didn't see a monster.

"There's no monster here," he said.
"Look!"

"It was a trick," laughed Kipper.
"It was just a trick!"

Dad laughed, and tucked Kipper up.
"Be a good boy and go to sleep," he
said. "And no more tricks!"

Floppy was hiding. He didn't like
monsters.

"Come out, Floppy," said Dad. "Kipper
is going to sleep."

But Kipper wasn't going to sleep. He was still wide awake.

"I don't like being on my own," he grumbled. "It's boring."

Kipper laughed. "I know! I'll play another trick," he said. "I'll trick Mum and get her to come upstairs."

"Mum!" yelled Kipper. "There's a hairy-scary monster! It's going to eat me up. Mum, help!"

Mum ran up to Kipper's bedroom.
Floppy barked and ran after her.

"What monster?" said Mum. "Where
is it?"

Kipper pointed to the wardrobe. "It's in the wardrobe," he said. "It's got long sharp claws and hairy jaws."

Mum looked in the wardrobe, but
she didn't see a monster.

"There's no monster here," she said.
"Look!"

"It was a trick!" laughed Kipper. "It was just a trick."

Mum tucked Kipper up again. "Be a
good boy and go to sleep," she said.
"And no more tricks!"

Kipper began to fall asleep. His
eyes were just closing when he heard
something under the bed.

It was something that was snuffling.
It was something that was snorting.
It was something that was hairy and
very, very scary!

"Help!" yelled Kipper. "There really is a monster! Mum, Dad, help me! I'm scared!"

Mum and Dad ran upstairs.

"What's wrong, Kipper?" they said.

"There's a monster," he sobbed.

"There's a monster under the bed."

Dad looked under the bed.

"There is a monster!" he said. "It's
the Hairy-Scary Floppy Monster!"

Talk about the story

Why didn't Kipper want to go to sleep?

Which three places did Kipper say the monster was hiding?

What things made you laugh in the story?

What makes you scared?

Hide and Seek

What is the monster hiding from? Find the words that rhyme. The words that are left tell you what the monster is hiding from.

claws

trick

hairy

man

mouse

little

pan

stick

jaws

scary

Remembering the stories together

Encourage your child to remember and retell the stories in this book. You could ask questions like these:

- Who are the characters?
- What happens at the beginning?
- What happens next?
- How does the story end?
- What was your favourite part? Why?

Story prompts

When talking to your child about the stories, you could use these more detailed reminders to help them remember the exact sequence of events. Turn the statements below into questions, so that your child can give you the answers. For example, *What does Gran see on the beach? What do the men want to do?* And so on …

Dolphin Rescue

- Gran sees the dolphin on the beach.
- Some men see the dolphin, too, and want to pull it back into the sea.
- Gran tells them to leave it alone and calls for help.
- Wilma keeps all of the children away.
- The rescue team get the dolphin back in the sea safely.

Gran's New Blue Shoes

- Gran is going to meet the Queen.
- Gran needs to choose a new outfit.
- When she gets to the palace, the heel on Gran's new shoe comes off.
- Chip runs up to a car driving past and asks the Duke for help.
- They wait by the gate as someone brings Gran some new blue shoes from the palace.
- The Queen likes Gran's new shoes!

118

Husky Adventure

- Floppy doesn't want to play, so he hides in Biff's bedroom.
- The magic key takes Floppy on an adventure.
- He is taken to a cold and snowy forest.
- Some wolves growl at Floppy and chase him.

- A man asks Floppy to help pull his sled with his husky dogs.
- The husky dogs can't keep up with Floppy!

Hairy-Scary Monster

- Kipper doesn't want to go to sleep.
- He tricks Mum and Dad and shouts that there is a hairy-scary monster.
- Dad looks and can't see any monsters.
- Mum looks in the wardrobe and can't see any monsters.

- Then Kipper really hears something under his bed.
- But it's only Floppy!

You could now encourage your child to create a 'story map' of each story, drawing and colouring all the key parts of them. This will help them to identify the main elements of the stories and learn to create their own stories.

Authors and illustrators

Dolphin Rescue written by Roderick Hunt, illustrated by Nick Schon
Gran's New Blue Shoes written by Roderick Hunt, illustrated by Nick Schon
Husky Adventure written by Roderick Hunt, illustrated by Alex Brychta
Hairy-Scary Monster written by Cynthia Rider, illustrated by Alex Brychta

OXFORD
UNIVERSITY PRESS

Great Clarendon Street, Oxford, OX2 6DP, United Kingdom

Oxford University Press is a department of the University
of Oxford. It furthers the University's objective of excellence
in research, scholarship, and education by publishing
worldwide. Oxford is a registered trade mark of Oxford
University Press in the UK and in certain other countries

Husky Adventure, *Dolphin Rescue*, *Gran's New Blue Shoes* text © Roderick Hunt 2005, 2008
Hairy-Scary Monster text © Cynthia Rider 2006

Husky Adventure, *Hairy-Scary Monster* illustrations © Alex Brychta 2005, 2006
Dolphin Rescue, *Gran's New Blue Shoes* illustrations © Alex Brychta and Nick Schon 2008

The characters in this work are the original creation of Roderick Hunt
and Alex Brychta who retain copyright in the characters

The moral rights of the authors have been asserted

Husky Adventure first published in 2005
Hairy-Scary Monster first published in 2006
Dolphin Rescue, *Gran's New Blue Shoes* first published in 2008

This Edition published in 2018

British Library Cataloguing in Publication Data
Data available

ISBN: 978-0-19-276423-2

10 9 8 7 6 5 4 3 2 1

Paper used in the production of this book is a natural, recyclable product
made from wood grown in sustainable forests. The manufacturing process
conforms to the environmental regulations of the country of origin.

Printed in China

Acknowledgements

Series Editors: Annemarie Young and Kate Ruttle